****

Under an Emotive Sky

By: Kathleen Hoctor-Bieler

****

Table of Content

Bully on My Mind

What is it that you were thinking, as you climbed the cold, damp steel?

Did all my taunts and sneers, make you try so hard not to feel,

The sharp shards that tore into your heart, as you climbed higher on each wrung.

Did I make you feel less than human, when I said how you did not belong?

Did you cry yourself to sleep each night, while planning a plot?

To end the crushing pain, so to never again have a sorrowful thought.

And high above the water below, did you pause a moment on the brink of nevermore?

Did you see my face; did you play back my words, before you hit the cold, sea floor?

Sounds, Sounds, Sounds....

The sounds of life reflect my mood,

Go round & round; happy & glad, sad & blue.

Haunting train whistle, the sound, rolling thru my mind,

From a not so distant town, feeling lonely and left behind.

Church bells on a Sunday morning, too many years ago.

Lifting spirits, while soaring above the memories in tow.

Crickets that go clickity- click on a sultry, September night.

Through silent, sullen breezes, under a starry, sky so bright.

Rustling of the crackling leaves, by winds that heaven sent.

Are the sounds that reflect my mood, as I silently lament.

Angels I Have Known

I felt your overwhelming presence...

Nudging me almost off my feet.

Arming me with your grace,

Knocking me from a paralyzed state.

Sight be told, there may be no tomorrow,

And silence roars back at me, Do it now,

Or bring ceremony for all your sorrows.

Gripped by the teeth, with unrelenting fear,

I hear the searing screams, it rises higher and higher.

The visceral vision rips thru the silent afternoon,

Bloody tears hit the ground loud, demanding …

Move your ass...Do it now!

Can't believe this is in front of me,

Doubting my eyes, questioning my ears,

When a guttural sound from deep inside,

Grasps tight my throat, throws my head back.

Eyes fixed upon the target,

The weapon soaring toward the task.

Furious whirling fur, screaming ball of fury,

Then silence, at last….

Picking up the broken pieces,

Huddled in my arms... the demon has passed.

Because

Because we are different, in loving bodies that are the same

We are looked down upon as causing others shame.

Why should it matter, it is not you I seek to change?

Carry on with your life, as Love has no name.

Love seeks to lighten, love lessens the load.

Be happy for Love, or be a part of what is wrong

With the world, all judging and hurting and

Not very nice. Live and let live, some good advice.

You would be more peaceful, if you would look toward the light.

Then you would see, Love could never be wrong, but always right.

As we Trek the Mountain High

Ralph & John, now long ago, gone,

By my side, day in, day out, in my shadow,

You hide...

In my heart, you sing a song,

As we trek the mountain, side by side,

So strong my grip, you have never died.

Your strength I feel in my every step.

With strong arms, my weariness you support,

My grasp...

Years ago, I thought you left,

But here today, it is not just a memory,

I thank...

You carry me further, until I can rest

Between you, where I will sit

Upon the river bank...with you both

Amen my Sons....

Friends To The End

Life is grand, but fleeting.

A perfect blend and meeting

Of Souls...together from the beginning.

On journeys, with paths that cross

Through the test of time, with love and loss.

And hearts still beating without pause,

To know we linger with each other to the end

Of time, you remain my friend that never bends

Through crooked roads and valleys deep.

With laughter and tears, we stumble in

Across the years, until that lofty place we view.

Then, hand-in-hand will climb, a stairway to heaven
with you.

Funeral for a Seed....All Glory Be.

As sweet Spring winds propel the seed,

Up, down; finally, dropping to its knees.

Crushing dirt upon its head.

Covered in silence, playing dead.

Then coached along from out its slumber,

Beating heart, through depths far under.

Remember the promise, remain not asunder.

Quiet now, seeking solace, it begins to wonder, when...

Suddenly, can gently feel upon its searching head,

Dancing raindrops, before the light is shed.

Alas! A tiny quiver, an itch to its timber.

A mighty stretch from sleep, now limber.

Wisdom provokes knowledge, less is always more.

Astoundingly, from smothering dirt, to the sky it soars!

Cause it is all about the seed,

Dropping to its knees.

Crushing dirt upon its head.

Covered in silence, playing dead....

HOMELESS

She lived in the house for 40 years plus.

Sitting daily upon her porch...watching a world she used to trust.

After 3 children, and 16 grandchildren reared.

She lovingly reminisced, every thought she held dear.

She spoke softly about a time gone by,

When working in a factory was her daily grind.

Her life was hard with much blood, sweat, and tears.

But life was generally sweet and good to her, over the years.

She buried two husbands, and spoke of them often.

Eighty years on her face, made her smile and voice soften.

As she spoke of the City people, who said she must leave,

Her home of 40 years and all the memories she will grieve.

Long after they evicted her and locked the door tight,

She returned daily, to sit on its stoop, long into the night.

Her sadness was heavy; surrounded by thoughts, full of regret.

Still day after day, she sat with the memories, she could never forget.

The police car pulled up, the bulldozers not very far behind,

A few minutes more, she pleaded softly, if you would be ever so kind.

You see sir; this is my home, my heart, my peace of mind.

Please don't make me leave; for such another place, I never shall find.

Get in the car madam, this old house it must come down!

I cannot my dear sir, along with my memories; it is my only here and now.

As she relented and bent slowly to get into the car.

A tear dropped on her lap, as she gazed from afar.

The engines started on the bulldozers that would maim.

Her heart, her soul, her home, nothing left to remain.

As the hungry jaws maneuvered around each sheltering wall,

Of decades of children in times that past, its lot had been cast.

Down they all fell in a cloudy pile of dust, leaving her broken and hushed.

But as the car pulled away, she talked about a not so distant day,

Of happier times, when life for her was jubilant and full of grace.

She silently whispered, the house may be gone, the memories will never erase.

Mansions They Can't Destroy

When the last of the bricks and concrete fell,

I knew your time was marked, I knew

Your days on this earth were fading fast,

I knew, your glory days had passed....

The tears you spilled on a broken ground,

Upon your Holy Sanctuary brought down, while

Leaving the yellow dust to settle on an empty lot.

Now your bones lay peacefully in a new plot.

Your voice still calls to me from across the way,

Where I scattered wildflower seeds, to fill the empty space.

One day I will pick them from the lot that was your home,

And bring them to you once again, to adorn your silent grave....

Farewell, My Sweet Friend, Ida Mae,

Your mansion now, they can never touch.

No cranes to dismember your sweet memories,

Just sweet flowers to smell from the settled, yellow dust.

In The World, Not of It

Sometimes the world is not very nice.

But remember, it is not your real home.

And grace alone leads you out, never looking back twice,

Over this place you have traveled, from dark into light.

Grey clouds are important, contrasting as they do.

Making sunsets and sunrises a glorious hue...

So, glide through this time here in this place

Fully aware, your home in paradise is what waits....

If I Die Today

Not sure how to spend this day,

Run ahead or pause to play.

Call my family and my friends,

Or pray alone, until the end.

Ponder up memories of old.

So grandchildren can be told,

Of all the glorious days, I have spent.

Even some I have lived to regret.

Overall, I would like them to recall,

And smile thinking, she has done it all.

Mostly though, take example of the last.

She would do it all again, if ever asked...maybe!

Not FEAR, But FAITH

Fear is not real, only something we create.

When we think we are out of time, think we are running late.

There is no fear in heaven, as all the bread has leavened.

Taking our blinders down, it is only truth that is found.

Then, it is scary for a reason, forcing change, like with the seasons.

As you shed the heavy, winter clothes, it is then that you suppose.

It's only the rolling stone that knows, looking back as it goes.

At all the pretty flowers, that in its stead has grown.

Rainbow Journey

Though the journey is always here and now.

The only thing that matters is all about the 'how'.

The mission is to do our best, each and every day.

Knowing God will guide us along the bumpy way.

The days turn into months and the months into years.

Yesterday is gone; today and now is what is here.

To seize the moment as it comes, remembering it is short.

One-step, then the next is more than enough to absorb.

And when you come to the finish line of that long fought race.

Take a deep breath, wipe off the sweat and with a smiling face,

Remember the troubles as tiny in scope, drink in the sweet victory!

No longer just a hope, as you gaze at mansions, far as you can see.

You are home, yes, finally home; so forget the bumps and bruises,

All the scraped up knees, worth it all, as I recall, and a wild ride indeed!

Sometimes

Sometimes we get too close, to see the shadow or the smoke.

Sometimes it faintly whispers in your ear,

To run somewhere toward something, outta fear.

But wait, stand up tall and listen closely again...

It is the shadow of the smoke, which will remain your friend.

That calls your name, like wind thru the forest,

Pointing you the way toward a solace, you must trust.

Scattering the moments, like leaves, between some time and space.

Always as you look back, there is that special moment of grace.

That holds your hand through moments just like this,

And steely stiffens your spine, as it softens a heart that feels dismissed.

Then... before you know it, gripping grace comes to cradle that forgotten memory.

Of a God, that has held you closely through eons... You are so very loved!

RED WHITE

A man of sorrow, of beauty, of earths own delights.

Ethereal soul that haunts with words, he carries you into light.

With a heart, that transcends anything of this world

Makes dim the sun, the moon, and the stars of gold.

He lifts your heart onto pedestals, from out of the raging sea.

From where you can believe in yourself and all that you can be.

He sees the darkness, but searches out the light,

As the phoenix that soars from the bleakest of nights.

He reminds of the tomorrow that will forever come,

To the broken down soul, that has lost its glorious sun.

His legacy abounds from his words, his heart, and his very soul.

That gleams from auras somewhere beyond this broken world...

Sunset of my Day

Today is the last day, oh such decisions I must make.

Shall I foxtrot or sashay, am I asleep or awake?

Rhapsody in Blues and Raptures in Pink, wait a minute here,

False (profits) abound, deceiving many of you, I do think...

Remember, the hour be not known, Jesus did speak,

How the final day, with no warning, will stealth in as a thief.

Rather focus on living, as if it could be any day, and is

Indeed every day, soul dies to the self, along the way.

Sarayu to provide the wings, and other such things,

You will need for the great escape, worry is not one.

And it matters not, when the train leaves the station,

God alone knows the schedule, your ETA written in the stars,

From a long ago promise, made before the beginning of time.

When the moment comes to go home, God alone leads me by the arm.

The Last Breath

Upon a twisted, knurled plank of wood,

Stretched a Man between Evil and Good.

Two criminals abut His right and His left,

Precious blood dripping down His Holy chest.

A mission that ended, in a thankless quest.

How long must I lay here, prayers for a final breath...

Into Your Hands, I commend My Soul.

Inhaling the broken World, exhaling His Holy Spirit.

It is over now, the End, as He ascends to the Father,

With His last breath, He carries us home again.

The Forward Path

Age is but a number to mark the years in time.

It only really matters, when you look behind.

Time is like a runner, each minute passing fast.

So many of todays, surrendering to the past....

So keep your focus forward, each and every day.

Then life becomes a celebration; always on its way!

THE ADDICT

Body reduced to skeleton; eyes, to black holes already dead.

I will not do this tomorrow; I cannot do this again....

Looking like a shadow of something that has been.

Once alive, but under the poppy, skirting hell, never relief.

Pact with the devil, exchanged my body, mind and soul for,

Silent screams, circuitous thoughts, laconic, demonic beliefs.

Euphoric playground empty now, as the terse pendulum swung.

Into the land of Hades, miserable suffering; behold a life undone.

Written in Stone or Blown Away

When an utterance brings the echo,

The Word is already gone.

Long thru the oral cavity of saliva.

Hanging blithely from a far

Off place, a remnant often forgotten,

Between hanging participles,

And escape diagrams of time & space.

A Word is a word, until it is erased.

As a Promise sinks into prose,

A visionary cartoon to take its place,

Among hollow histories that stand alone,

Written in stone today, like sand tomorrow....

It is all blown away.

Dreams

In case you forget, in case ya didn't know...

I count your every breath

As you sleep beside me, your heart's rhythm,

Lulls me to sleep, as we soar

Through tumbling, celestial clouds

Careful, never looking down

Instead, we dance through crystal starlight,

And ride the cow over the moon

Toward bright tomorrows, promising

To be here very soon.

Hurling through the Milky Way, two by two

Past galaxies that echo our names.

We giggle as we pinch the comet's tail,

Holding each other tight.

Then catapulted thru the quixotic sky.

Landing softly on lips,

That smile and caress my mouth, awake.

My eyes take in your sight.

Home again, beside me, I watch,

And count your every breath.

Morning is near, so I pull you closer.

Tomorrow is here....

Wishing Upon a Star

As the universe unfurls, there are oh such beauties in the world.

To but open my eyes and gaze upon a dark, dotted sky.

Reach up and pick any diamond from the heavenly perch,

Leaving a celestial hole, that now dances in my trembling hand.

Twinkling ball of energy. First a wish, a kiss, and then I blow you away.

You are free, to return to dance in a dark, holy sky.

A moment to ponder, before you shoot across a heavenly horizon,

To wander thru the spacious night, with my prayer under your wing

I watch you till you're outta sight; good-bye you wink.

Off to deliver my thoughts to a waiting God...

On and On....

Racing the Moon, hitching a star.

Seeing it all from a distance so far.

We live on, we live on....

Our thoughts are never gone.

Dreams of burning, tempest limbs,

And fractured whispers deep within.

Pounding hearts, sweated brow,

Sweet titillation's only you arouse.

We live on, we live on...

Our thoughts are never gone.

Our minds and bodies mingle and flow,

No matter how far away we go.

Like a hot summer breeze,

Still and Breathless, you linger on me.

Cause we live on, we live on...

Our thoughts are never gone.

Humming What Matters

Stay perfectly still and listen hard.

Do you hear the birds' song?

I hear it from my window,

I hear it from afar...

The crickets too, late though they chirp.

Both sing a haunting note.

Above the din of traffic, rushing around,

There is a greater sound...

Just be still, and you will know,

The quelled fear of your beating heart.

Close your eyes and you can tell,

Where you end and where you start.

Please, linger long and repeat your song,

Until I can hum it all day long.

Time

Withered, diminutive morsel of time,

Weakened pinion, slowly unwinds.

Adroitly tending both rhythm and rhyme,

Following your finite 'state of mind'.

Selected soliloquy, one senses the fear.

Peering your clocks, we strain to hear,

Whispers of warnings, lamps keep trimmed.

Belies the brevity, which lies within.

Entropic remnants, echoing what's been.

Tinges of memories, blowing in the wind.

Of a something, sometime, or maybe has been.

Fickle fella, sentient soul; friend, yet foe be told.

Teacher of lessons, written on the heart.

Be your message, your mission, your work of art.....

Celebrating Spring

Heady, odoriferous equinox.

Time to take off your winter socks.

Chartreuse, green faced willow,

You have returned, good fellow.

Chin up! Brave little daffodils,

Perched on lovely, golden hills.

Busy, boisterous birds...up before dawn,

Never to rest, beaking straw to your nest.

Bees come again alive, smelling sweet nectar,

As they fly, searching for flowers, glorious lecterns,

From where to deliver another new chance.

To pollinate dreams, and follow the dance,

Of birds, and bees, and flowers and trees,

Telling of Spring and other glorious
things....Welcome!

The Moon

Haughty moon, marauder of hearts, masterpiece in the sky.

Glowingly sullen, with a presence of oneness you belie.

Abundance of haze, floating in the sky so dark.

Waxing or waning, you cling to your phase.

Tides obey, wolves howl, obliquely straddling the earth you embrace.

Nocturnal is your nightly grace, quest of ethereal countenance.

A visage of delight, you light the world,

Crazies tripped, lunacies warped; Oh, sensual girl.

Night falls to day; shaded, you slowly become.

Vampires retire, werewolves stand mute,

As you close your eye, day surrenders,

Again, you shine, upon your throne on high....

Feels Right

Fighting the urge to remain alone, but oh sweet night.

Your words are whispers, your body feels right.

There are no yesterdays to think of, only soft gazes,

And your gentle touch, trembles and amazes,

Me in ways you probably can guess, in spite,

Of fears that reach for me, your body feels right.

When you are near to me, we breathe in unison.

We leave the rest behind, our dream has just begun.

Close my eyes now, you will still be here,

In the morning, whispering my name.

Pulling me near, breathing in sweet delight.

Trembling, reminding me, your body feels right.

The Big Picture

I am a glorious child, made from one morsel of God.

Raise me with love and care, but spare not the rod.

Just an everyday story, floating with the ebbing tide.

A single scrap of driftwood, trying to enjoy the ride.

Being in the big picture, but only one piece of the puzzle.

Fitting in just the right place, in this specific time and space.

Fit me in amongst the others...knowing there is not another,

Who will complete this work of art, which our Creator chose to start.

If I were instead a lengthy book, then but a chapter I would be.

Read along with the others, a wondrous novel to be seen.

But if instead I was a tune, a single note of music heard,

Amidst the melodies in the air, orchestras resound everywhere!

This picture would become a masterpiece of gold.

And this book would be a classic story told,

In history books of Art and Lit. , such beauty to behold.

As all the bits and pieces come together as they mold,

A Universe, a summation of One, combining all the others,

Into the sacred Soul of Old, God's plan is done and story told.

Times Are A Changin'

Bombs in Times Square; Ole Opry, water everywhere.

Thrown out of school for wearing the American flag,

Oil in our seas choke our fish and make them gag.

Sick birds on our shores gasp, please NO more.

Greedy worms on Wall St. gamble on food
commodity markets,

Increases global hunger, up to 130 million more it
targets.

Earthquakes rain down around us, like late afternoon
thunder.

Tornadoes rip and roar thru the streets, taking many
asunder.

More people out of work, swelling unemployment
lines.

Foreclosures lay empty, dotting our countryside.

These times are all around us, forget them, we might
try.

Turn off the T.V's, and all the newspapers we will
hide.

Will we remember to heed the warnings of long ago?

Or stare straight ahead, without admitting what we all
know?

www.ingramcontent.com/pod-product-compliance
Lightning Source LLC
Chambersburg PA
CBHW030310030426
42337CB00012B/656